Happy

♡ love you so
much!
Aunt Michelle

"In *Ash and Starlight*, Arianne Lehn enters life fully, bringing all it contains into her relationship with the Holy. Here you will find tender prayers resonant with hope, the kind that sail freely on days of joy and stay afloat during times of turmoil. No matter what kind of day you've had, there's a prayer waiting for you."
　　— Joyce Rupp, author of *Praying Our Goodbyes* and
　　　Open the Door

"Ours is a time when the voice of faith—with its claims, its risks, and its daring—must be articulated with venturesome freshness. Arianne Lehn responds to that requirement and here offers a rich catalogue of prayers that are open, inviting, and elusive enough for many entry points. Her imaginative probes are deeply linked to scripture, playful enough to be a fitting match for the playfulness of scripture. It is exactly, as she says in her subtitle, a moment for grace and chaos. Those who engage this book will find courage for chaos and receptivity for grace."
　　— Walter Brueggemann, Columbia Theological Seminary

"Arianne's prayers are crafted from the honest stuff of everyday life. Who of us has not felt messy, jealous, or on a threshold when old beliefs have died? This book meets you in the midst of all that glorious humanity, allowing you to bless the raw, challenging places and infuse them with grace so that you can see your reality in new ways. She offers the gift of potent words when sometimes we don't have our own to form."
　　— Christine Valters Paintner, author of *The Soul's Slow
　　　Ripening: 12 Celtic Practices for Seeking the Sacred* and a
　　　poetry collection, *Dreaming of Stones*

"Especially in these days when I find myself saying 'I have no words' on a regular basis, Arianne Lehn offers the words. Elegant, gorgeous words to calm our souls and ease our days. In addition to seasonal prayers, she addresses brokenness, insecurities, and doubts—all of which the world faces daily. *Ash and Starlight* offers a sigh of relief."
　　— Jan Edmiston, co-moderator of the Presbyterian Church
　　　(USA)

"In this lush collection of prayers, Arianne Braithwaite Lehn manages to speak in a voice that is equal parts lyrical and unflinchingly real. The complicated breadth of life's joys and challenges are reflected in the pages of this book. For those moments when the feelings are on the tip of your tongue but the words fail you, let these prayers be your guide and companion."
— MaryAnn McKibben Dana, author of *God, Improv, and the Art of Living* and *Sabbath in the Suburbs*

"At once beautifully poetic and relatable, *Ash and Starlight* glows. Braithwaite Lehn invites readers on a pilgrimage of prayer and into an awareness of God's abiding presence. Most of all, she welcomes us to share her words as we pray. Her many and varied ways to address the Divine—*Welcoming One, My Friend, Patient One*, and so many more—are especially moving."
— Jennifer Grant, author of *Love You More* and *Maybe I Can Love My Neighbor Too*

"As a busy working mom, I crave moments of spiritual connection but need to find them in the cracks of my everyday life. Arianne Lehn's book provides just the right words at just the right time. This book is perfect for setting on a bedside table and picking up for a prayer here and there, when I need it most. Written with tenderness and concern, *Ash and Starlight* is like having a spiritual director on call, to page whenever I need her."
— Traci Smith, author of *Faithful Families: Creating Sacred Moments at Home*

"Even with a shelf dedicated to prayer books and with journals and computer files filled with my own, *Starlight and Ash* is the prayer book I've been longing for. Lehn's gorgeous writing, her disciplined focus and yet wide-open spirit give us the words to pray when we're fresh out and lead us to ask for things we might not know we need. What a gift this book is! A must read for prayer 'warriors' and 'novices' alike."
— Caryn Rivadeneira, author of *Grit and Grace: Heroic Women of the Bible* and *Gritty and Graceful: 15 Inspiring Women of the Bible*

"Lehn's prayers address the painful times and seasons in our lives, when our faith and spirit are stretched to the breaking point. Her honesty and vulnerability give voice to our sighs and groans. Her prayers lift us back to our unsteady feet as we stumble forward in the darkness now grasping a glimpse of light. They draw us to the 'thin places'—spaces where the 'veil' between heaven and earth feels paper-thin, as Lehn herself so perfectly states.

Her writing is stunningly gorgeous. The words appear to pour from the pain through the pen. Yet it is obvious that every joining of consonant and vowel has been sifted through her spirit prior to being committed to the page.

Do not rush through the reading of these prayers. Savor each delicious word. Taste and see that the God of Light and Word is good, with us unceasingly, and forever. *Ash and Starlight: Prayers for the Chaos and Grace of Daily Life* is a collection to cherish, to share, to keep, to have as life's inevitable challenges stop us in our tracks."

— Kathleen Long Bostrom, author of *Who Is Jesus* and *What about Heaven?*

"Arianne Braithwaite Lehn has gifted us with a collection of prayers that spring from deep faith, sensitivity, and passion. We hear her authentic voice and feel her open heart as she writes with elegance, graceful expression, and moving beauty. These are prayers to empower and equip us. They are filled with fresh images and truly reach us in all seasons of our lives, as we call on our tender God, our merciful Jesus, and our supportive Spirit. This is a book to savor and share. Its prayers can strengthen our life-giving connection with God, helping us participate in prayerful dialogue that sustains and nourishes our days. This book is a blessing."

— Donald K. McKim, author of *Everyday Prayer with John Calvin* and *Mornings with Bonhoeffer: 100 Reflections on the Christian Life*

arianne
braithwaite
lehn

Ash &
Starlight

prayers for
the chaos
& grace of
daily life

chalice
press

Saint Louis, Missouri

An imprint of Christian Board of Publication

Cover design: Jennifer Pavlovitz
Cover art: Penelope Dullaghan, penny@penelopedullaghan.com

ChalicePress.com

Print ISBN: 9780827200807

EPUB: 9780827200814   EPDF: 9780827200821

For Dad —
You continue to pilgrimage
with me every day

Contents

Prayers for Guidance and Transition

Prayers for Waiting and Struggle

Prayers for Trust

Prayers for Comfort and Strength

Prayers for Seasonal and Liturgical Times of Year

Introduction

Every person is a pilgrim journeying toward a sacred place. While each faith tradition encompasses holy sites, there is a personal pilgrimage each one of us takes. And, that is to the most sacred place of all—the heart within.

Each morning, we begin a new leg of the journey toward what's deepest within us—a *Heart* planted within our own hearts meant to stir, guide, and comfort us in every way. Because we are God-breathed creatures infused with God's very essence, the further we go into our own truest heart, the further we go into God's.

At times, a pilgrim is a wanderer. Yet even when we lose sight of where we're headed or start to make a different destination for ourselves—a false identity, a shiny image, an empty promise—the pilgrimage remains seamless. The journey is still holy in all its detours and off-roading. Efficiency and perfection aren't the goals (of which I must remind myself daily).

My own soul connects deeply with the Celtic tradition. Celtic Christianity grounds itself in the goodness of the pilgrimage, the pilgrim, and the Holy One who created both. I resonate with the concept of "thin places"—spaces where the "veil" between heaven and earth feels paper-thin. These places exist in our everyday lives. They are also inside us.

The poetry of Genesis centers us with this. While God created us from the ash and dust of the earth, God then blew divine breath into us. This same breath created the stars—what ancient people saw as "heavenly beings" filled with transcendent, pure, and powerful beauty. The illumined meaning of the poem uncovers a beautiful truth. We are made of earth and we are made of heaven. Ash and starlight woven together.

And ash and starlight fill our journeys too. I was 31 weeks pregnant with my first child the day my father died. With one hand on my belly, I felt my baby kicking inside. With the other, I held Dad's fingers as he ran into Christ's arms.

Following my father's death, his brother commissioned a musical piece in remembrance—not just of my father, but of the message his life spoke. A heart in pilgrimage. It was a song of life's wounds and life's joys. My weary and grief-stricken surrender coupled with God's holy hands in producing the text for that piece. I called it "Ash and Starlight."

This piece would later become the collective title for my most intimate writing—my prayers. Early on in my ministry as a pastor, I began the practice of composing weekly prayers in which I incorporated prayer requests church members shared with me. It became a spiritual discipline through which my truest voice surfaced. When I needed to step away from parish ministry, I continued the practice of writing prayers through a blog titled "Ash and Starlight."

Prayer is how I pilgrimage through the dust and splendor of my own life. It involves expressing what's within me to God and listening for God's responses, questions, comfort, and challenges. There's always this conversation happening within my heart, regardless of whether or not I'm listening to it. Awareness of this dialogue draws me closer toward my journey's desire, awakens me to Love, and helps me know God more deeply.

Too often, I've thought I needed to remove parts of my life or myself in order to grow closer to God. I now see I do not need to "fix" anything—my surroundings or myself—in order to pray. I can go deeply into the heart of God anytime. My authentic voice and open heart are what I need, and those are things to which I always have access. Praying while I feed the baby, after I get off a tough phone call, or when I feel completely scattered are all experiences enveloped by God's presence.

I'm learning and relearning how the things needed to strengthen this sense of life-giving connection are not "out there," but within me. My everyday emotions, joys, and frustrations can be the most genuine times of prayer. The inner jumble of thoughts is itself prayer.

And, what I am trying to embrace is how all these everyday experiences matter for my pilgrimage—that where I am is okay, even *good.* Vibrant connection with God, with others, with my own self, is possible not in spite of, but because of, where I am right now. My faithfulness in this part of the pilgrimage will lead me to the next, and, all the while, I can channel God's blessing when I keep that passage open through prayer.

My hope for you, sibling pilgrim, is to find in these pages a prayerful companion for your own journey. This companion encompasses prayers for your inner landscape and outer rhythms. There are prayers for what you're feeling and prayers for the year's seasons.

These prayers may be starting spots for your own— a springboard you can use to offer to God your own unique thoughts and feelings you need to let loose. Or, these prayers can also be a place for you to rest. I have been so thankful for the prayers of others when I myself didn't have it in me to pray—or didn't want to.

Following each prayer are a few scripture references. These connect with the themes of the prayer and provide nourishment and wisdom for further meditation.

I pray you see how the experiences and emotions you want to leave behind are actually integral to who you are and are becoming. God wants your honest attention and availability more than piety and achievement.

I long for you to be grounded in the deepest promises of which we all need the most reminding: We are loved as we are. We are not alone. We are instruments of blessing, even when we don't realize it.

I hope you feel freshly empowered and equipped to approach life with grace and curiosity; to surrender and trust amid your fears; to rejoice in your current life, even as you're moving toward something else. You will uncover how all the seasons of your inner and outer life instrumentally form you.

May you awaken to sentiments you didn't realize were harbored within you, and invite God to share in them. And, may you say yes to the ash and starlight in your journey, because there is no transformative power in what we deny.

The world is a broken and beautiful place, and a tender, strong God holds us in it. I pray you find connection and wholeness as you run with elation or crawl on hands and knees through the dark. We will all do both.

We won't fully reach the destination—at least, not in this life. But God will give us glimpses along the way—enough to get us up in the morning and say "yes" all over again. On we go.

* * *

Ash and Starlight

On waves where trembling feet
Sink and dance there rises
Between my toes a peace...
Where heaven and earth embrace,
Where the ash in my mouth,
The starlight in my bones,
Weave together in wholeness.

I run
Carried on a strength beyond me,
Feet raging against soil I did not choose.
My eyes turn upward,
And through the grit, the tears, the joy
Long to glimpse the land of the living.

I sing
Adding my voice to the universal chorus.
Turning my song from a plea for deliverance
To a chord of gratitude.

I love
Unfurling my hands in aching yes
And clasp the holy gift,
Which is this day,
Which is enough.
Another chance to live,
To burn with grace. [†]

—2015, text by Arianne Braithwaite Lehn,
musical composition by Timothy C. Takach

A Short Note on How and to Whom I Pray

While I definitely don't believe prayer must begin with, "Dear God," or end with, "Amen," it can be a comforting framework, collecting me into place when I feel distracted, confused, and stressed. I don't always pray this way. Sometimes, all I can do is groan. Sometimes, I close my eyes and smile. Sometimes, I turn on a piece of music, letting it form the prayers of my heart. And, sometimes, I focus on my breath, remembering it is God's life-force right there.

I have long found comfort in Romans 8:26–27, which promises, "[T]he Spirit helps us in our weakness...[interceding] with sighs too deep for words. And God, who searches the heart, knows what is the mind of the Spirit, because the Spirit intercedes for the saints according to the will of God."

The further I travel on my personal pilgrimage, the more God has expanded my embrace of both new vision and mystery. I celebrate the ever-growing variety of forms, images, and names by which God connects with us. I am deeply grateful to Joyce Rupp (*Fragments of Your Ancient Name*) and Lauren Winner (*Wearing God*) for their profound impact in broadening and deepening my love for the many ways we encounter God.

However I pray, and whatever words I use, I do so in the spirit and loving kindness of Christ—my *Home*.

Prayers for
Centering

When I need perspective at the start of the day

In this day, O God,

May I be alert.
May I be kind.
May I be compassionate.
May I be authentic,
May I be generous.
May I be forgiving.
May I be honest.
May I be brave.
May I be forgiving (again).
May I be open.
May I be creative.
May I be strong.
May I live from my intentions,
not simply my habits.

And may I hold closely in
prayer the people
you bring to my heart
and mind right now...

May I focus,
may I trust,
and, above all,
may I be yours.

Amen.

---

*Micah 6:8 * Romans 12:9–15 * Colossians 3:12–17*

> "[A]nd what does the LORD require of you
> but to do justice, and to love kindness,
> and to walk humbly with your God?"
> —*Micah 6:8*

When I need to get back to the basics

Tender One,

How blessed I am, God, to have
your love, your peace, your reassurance—
you give me the comfort I need
to live my hardest days.

How blessed I am, God, to have
your strength, your courage, your self-control—
you give me the grit I need
to make tough decisions and follow through.

How blessed I am, God, to have
your grace, your forgiveness, your promise of new life—
you give me the mercy I need
to say, "I'll make different choices today,"
and then do so.

You see me, God, as I truly am—
the core that's been there since
I was a baby and blossomed as a child.

A core buried beneath all of these layers.
A layer of responsibility here and layer of image there...
the layers of expectations others place on me...
the layers of self-doubt and fear.

Please help me shed the layers, God,
and return to the core.

Help me reclaim who I truly am—
the person you've created me to be.

May I live boldly,
speak confidently,
love unconditionally,

forgive readily,
and trust deeply.

Shape my life to match my soul.

With refreshed honesty
about myself and my heart,
I thank you for loving me as I am.

I embrace my true essence
and your work for me today.

Amen.

---

*Psalm 139:13 * Philippians 4:19 * 2 Timothy 1:6*

"[R]ekindle the gift of God that is within you..."
—2 Timothy 1:6

When I'm completely scattered

Centering and calming God,

Sometimes my mind is
both everywhere and nowhere at all.

I'm filled with such a mess of tasks,
reminders, and to-do alerts,
all pinging against the walls of my head.

I ask for your peace-giving guidance
to place these thoughts
where they ought to be today.

Every tiny thing in my life
looms seemingly large,
while the assignments,
relationships, and worries
engulf me.

Help me put aside what can wait,
letting what needs my attention
receive action it deserves.

Help me sort this out.

Slow down my breathing,
reminding me when
I've been a ball of anxiety before
and you've untangled
my life, my worries...

Give me space to remember these things
zipping within are not my life,
but small slices of it—
I'll take them on as I'm able,
one at a time (with you by my side).

With your holy breath, clear my mind...
With your purifying Spirit, cleanse my soul...
With your gentle presence, calm my heart...

Help me, God, in the confusion or the jumble
to focus on what really, really, matters.

Thank you for the ways you
center me and bring me back to life—
to the real, the important, the true.

May I go about the rest of this day
focused on you and grounded in your peace—
peace deeper than my understanding.

Amen.

*Isaiah 26:3 * Matthew 6:33 * Philippians 4:6–7*

"Those of steadfast mind you keep in peace—
in peace because they trust in you."
—Isaiah 26:3

When I'm a paradox of feelings

Sweet Spirit,

How grateful I am for
your companionship
in all I feel and hold.

Sometimes I feel unglued,
going in so many directions
and yearning for centeredness
amid the clamor.

Sometimes I feel bored stiff,
weighed down by the
heavy sameness of
my days and my choices.

Sometimes I feel strong and grateful,
amazed at the sweetness
in this season of life.

Sometimes I feel self-pitying,
sad that another week passed
without a phone call from family
or invitation from a friend.

Sometimes I feel consumed with worry—
people who need help,
people making sad choices,
people I feel responsible for,
people I don't understand
(or don't understand me).

You beautifully seam my paradoxes,
grounding both my
flurry and emptiness,
my worry and joy,
in your heart.

Help me give each of
these feelings their place—
to honor them,
accept them,
and with a breath of release,
blow away the ones no longer needed.

I praise you, Loving Spirit,
for the fresh energy and freedom you offer.
Thank you for living within me,
breathing your peace and power
into the bottom of my being.

It is not by my own abilities but by you
that I live out my calling.
I ask for your support to be with me,
for you are my Source of true strength.

You have been and will be with me —
in the variety of unique
circumstances and challenges I face.
I open my arms and eyes
with the acceptance you're teaching me…

Amen.

*Psalm 20:7 * Psalm 41:12 * Zechariah 4:6*

"You know me inside and out, you hold me together…"
                    —Psalm 41:12 (The Message)

14

When I need to ground myself in today

Calming One,

I am stopping now.
I am resting now.
I am letting the stillness
of being with you
wash in like a wave,
while the chatter and
activity around me recede.

Thank goodness I don't need
silence around me
in order to have quiet inside.

This moment, God—
it's what I need and where I am.

I find myself so encumbered
by yesterdays and tomorrows
that, sometimes, I leave today
in the corner.

But today is enough.

You're giving me the daily bread I need for now—
a person who loves me,
a moment to breathe,
a meal on the table,
a word bringing hope,
a gleam of life outside my window.

Please help me open my hands
and receive today with gratitude,
letting past seasons fill me with appreciation,
and seasons yet to be give me hope.

But, for now—
Today. Today. Today.

I love you best when I'm present,
seeing and hearing and holding
what asks for my heartfelt attention
here and now.

You promise to hold
space for everything else.

Thank you for bringing me back, God.
Thank you for the miracle of manna.

Amen.

---

1 Kings 17:8–16 * Matthew 6:11 * Matthew 6:34

"Give us this day our daily bread." —Matthew 6:11

When I'm at the end of a hard week

Guide of mind,
Companion of my heart...

You bring me gifts of solace and
encouragement at the close of another week.

Some events bruised my heart,
some discouraged my hopes,
some pierced me with panic,
some caused me to shut down...

And so, God, it is grace—it is gift—it is life—
that you welcome me with love,
meeting my soul in its most tender spot.

You come to me in my longing and my angst
as I process the week or wonder
how long I'll face these circumstances.

When my temptation, gentle God,
is to ask, "When?" or, "How long?"
collect my breathing in a
centered rhythm absorbed
with this moment—
focused on you and your goodness.

Use all I've experienced this week, God,
to help me break open and bloom.

Amen.

*Joshua 1:9 * Psalm 23:4 * Isaiah 42:3*

"I hereby command you: Be strong and courageous; do not be frightened or dismayed, for the LORD your God is with you wherever you go." —Joshua 1:9

When I need to see the beauty before me

Creator God,

You make everything beautiful in its time.

Please open my soul, Awakening One,
to the surprising beauty
(and timing!)
of this season.

I need you to draw me
in from my distraction.

I want to witness your brightness in
the greening earth and birds' song
as well as the neighbor walking past
or the child's sidewalk chalk.

I want to pause in awe at
the burning bushes in my
friend's well-timed email
or the stranger's unexpected kindness...
The line in my book that awakens my soul
or the masterful frost pattern
on my kitchen window.

I want to journey through this day
with an awareness bringing
gratitude and celebration—
fresh hope in what you're creating
and new eyes for the
treasure buried beneath me.

You promise that birth and death,
planting and harvest,
embrace and solitude

all have their place in
this world and my life.
A beautiful faith allows
things to unfold,
and grabs onto the
grace of daily glimpses.

Loving God, I rest in you
and your working to make
all things beautiful—
someday, somehow.

You are the One
who showed true
beauty in human life.

Amen.

*Exodus 3:2 * Psalm 8 * Ecclesiastes 3:1–11*

"For everything there is a season, and a time for every matter under heaven." —Ecclesiastes 3:1

When I need to stop ruminating

Nurturer toward my every need,

Bring my thoughts back
to you right now.

Ground my focus in
your promises to me.

Pull the roots of my gaze deep into
the nourishing soil of who you are.

I've been stuck in other soil...
seeds of thought
lie lodged in places of
anger over what's not fair,
anxiety over what might happen,
guilt over what just happened,
fear over the free fall.

Plant my groundless mind
with all its seedlings back in you,
the Soil feeding the best of me
for the needs of this world.

Instead of dwelling on what I'm owed,
I will celebrate all I have in you.

Instead of fearing whether I am enough,
I will celebrate the ways I am because of you.

Instead of wondering
(with a lot of hand-wringing!)
about the future,
I will celebrate how it
rests in your hands.

Even as this place of
underground germination is dark,
I will be at peace,
with my heart steadfast.

Amen.

*Mark 4:13–20 * 2 Corinthians 10:10 * Philippians 4:8*

"[W]hatever is true, whatever is honorable, whatever is just, whatever is pure, whatever is pleasing, whatever is commendable, if there is any excellence and if there is anything worthy of praise, think about these things." —Philippians 4:8

When I need some steadiness

Supportive Spirit,

You are the warmth around me,
the hope within me,
the resolve that leads me forward.

You bring light to my darkness,
and right now I'm longing
for that light to shine in the shadows
plaguing me most.

Please bring your faithful steadiness
to my life so often in flux.

Just as I think things are under control,
the trusted ground begins to shift,
my relationships rumble,
my insecurity starts erupting.

Not many things are dependable
in this life, God.

You are.

I declare my need for you
and trust in you.
Please be a Rock to
which I can cling,
even with shaky hands—
even with only a few fingers.

May I fix my eyes on you,
even as I don't know all
the surprises in store.

Help me look to you, God, in this day.
You are steady.
You are sure.

And, so is the light you promise
to shine on the next step before me.

Amen.

---

*1 Samuel 2:2 * Psalm 119:105 * Proverbs 3:5–6*

"Trust in the LORD with all your heart,...
and [God] will make straight your paths."
—Proverbs 3:5–6

When I'm heading to work

God, my Light,

Make me your lamp today.

Anoint these efforts of mine,
done for you,
done from love.

Shine in my thoughts.

Illumine my words.

Warm through my hands.

Shimmer in my speaking.

Beam from my priorities.

Glow in my countenance.

Sparkle through the stewardship
of my skills and desires.

Burn through my dedication in
parts of the job I don't want to do.

Please use me, God,
and bless this work.

I commit to faithfulness in
my tasks today, knowing
greatness comes not
through what is achieved,
but how it is done.

And, who knows what
hope you will reveal
through a small candle today...

Amen.

*Matthew 5:14–16 * John 8:12 * Colossians 3:23*

"You are the light of the world... Let your light shine before others, so that they may see your good works and give glory to [God] in heaven." —Matthew 5:14a, 16

Prayers for
Confession and
Release

When I want to numb, avoid, and block

Patient, gentle God,

I can be so afraid of emptiness.

There are many ways to swallow
the echoes of hollowness...
fill the house with unneeded stuff,
fill the wallet with money,
fill the garages with spares of this and that,
fill the belly with more and more food,
fill the mind with whatever distractions can be found,
fill the time with busy-ness...

But, it won't pad the emptiness
or fill the void.

Give me the courage, God,
to clear this clutter!

To see in this empty space
a sacredness,
a needed gift,
a place you will come
and get to work.

Make me be alone with you
and the things within
I've been avoiding
(or not even aware of).

Use this open space to
bring about transformation
in which your Spirit
shapes my attitudes,
leads my thoughts,

guides my decisions,
covers my conversations.

You promise that
to be filled with your Spirit
is to be in process—
always moving in
abundant purposefulness.

With your Spirit in me,
I am never empty,
nor is my life.

Fill and form me, Loving One, today.

Remind me I have all I need
in and through you,
and that there is
no reason to be afraid.

Amen.

John 14:16–17 * 1 Corinthians 3:16 * Ephesians 5:18

"Do you not know that you are God's temple and that God's Spirit dwells in you?" —1 Corinthians 3:16

When I'm struggling to accept my life right now

Completely Gracious One,

Forgive me.

I've slipped into cynicism this week,
hanging my heart on negativity
rather than hope,
covering bloody wounds
rather than opening them
to the air of your healing.

Air can sting.

I've been asking you
for a change in my circumstances.
And I've been complaining.

Sometimes, you want a
change of conditions,
and you equip me to
make that happen.

But maybe what
I need this time
is not a change of what's around me,
but a change *inside me*.

My heart,
not my circumstances.

Maybe a change in heart
will lead to a change
in circumstances?

But, for now, the changed
heart will be enough.

Instead of discontent, *gratitude.*
Rather than jealousy, *generosity.*
In place of judgment, *compassion.*
Replacing anger, *laughter.*

Mold my heart, God, into
the form you want it to be.
Lead me to my courage.
Kindle and warm what
has grown cold in me.
Energize the passions
lying lethargic.

In this day, help me stand
before all of my life
with a trusting, open heart.
That's a good enough change for now.
I will ask you about
those circumstances later.

I praise you as
the heart-renewing
God who is good,
the God who is able,
the God I love,
and the God of us all.

Amen.

---

*Psalm 34:10 * 2 Corinthians 12:9–10 * Philippians
4:11–13*

"[T]hose who seek the LORD lack no good thing..."
                                              —Psalm 34:10b

When I'm bound up in jealousy

Generous God,

You've created a universe of infinite blessing.
You never stop creating good.
The reserves are endless.

So, why have I made such
a small house for my heart,
with windows tinted by envy?

I look out and see
the gifts in others' lives,
and I am angry.

It's shameful.
And embarrassing.

But, this is the view from my tiny house,
whose walls are greed
and whose foundation is fear—
if they have this,
I won't, or can't, or will have less.

With your hands around mine,
I hold the lie at a further distance,
observing it for what it is,
letting it teach me the road
my heart has yet to travel,
the heart-house needing a remodel.

With patience,
non-judgment, and
relentlessly gentle love,
you never stop telling me, God,
of the freedom there is in celebration,

rather than competition.
Of the ever-expanding joy!
With you, blessing has no limit.

My cup runneth over...

Outside the window, I see the
jealousy, envy, insecurity, threats—
they turn to a mist now swallowed
by the rumbling storm of your voice.

You invite me outside into a
strong, cleansing rain
bringing my soul to rebirth.

Today I will give thanks
for the goodness I witness in others' lives,
believing it illumines a gracious God
and universe whose core is goodness.

I will mark with joy the flourishing I see.

With a huge exhale of
relief and anticipation,
I will step through the
threshold of my
new house.

Amen.

Psalm 23:5 * Luke 12:15 * 1 Thessalonians 5:16–18

*"Rejoice always, pray without ceasing, give thanks in all
circumstances..." —1 Thessalonians 5:16–18a*

When I need forgiveness and to forgive

Compassionate Creator,

You hold me with faithfulness each day,
and I'm asking for your
forgiveness to flood my life.

I recognize in myself persistent struggles...
the same old failures...
the things I get too tired to confess again...
the things I've hidden for so long
I've convinced myself they're
not so wrong after all.

Thank you for your patience, God.
Please forgive and free me.
Heal my heart and
liberate my mind.

Reveal to me, Lord, those I need to forgive.
From your reservoir of grace,
may new springs of healing and forgiveness
flow into my relationships.

Carve in me a deeper kindness.
May the pain others caused—
even pain they don't know about—
teach me a compassion
I would not have learned otherwise.

Loosen the hard, rigid bars
I've put around my heart,
and relax my expectations
with your humility and love.

Nurture a supportive space in me,
that I might give others a soft place
to land with sore hearts—
just as you've done, God, for me.

I pray that all I speak,
all I do,
all I dream,
and all I confess today
declare my love for you,
need for you,
and commitment to follow
your way, Lord.

Amen.

*Matthew 6:12 * Luke 6:36 * Romans 8:1–2*

"There is therefore now no condemnation for those who are in Christ Jesus... Jesus has set you free from the law of sin and death." —Romans 8:1–2

When I need a fresh spirit

Holy God,

Unfurl, unclench,
release, relax
my soul this day.

Unwind the tangled thoughts
that have trapped me
in webs of worry this week.

Show me I'm not cornered
in the decisions I face.

Bring my heart, mind,
conversations, and circumstances
into alignment as I seek to
keep putting one foot in front of the other...
peeling back the layers, one at a time,
to the person you've made me to be,
to the pieces of you placed within me.

I want to live with integrity, Lord—
to be whole on my inside and outside
and honest about my motives.

I hunger to hold quiet courage—
to be so steady in your promises
that I stop getting caught in comparison.

I need to see myself the way you do—
beloved and cherished and
completely enough.

Please, Holy Spirit, release my fear,
ushering into its place
new trust, confidence, and peace.

May I claim that spirit of power,
love, and self-discipline today
as I offer my life to you and your purpose.

As I follow your beckoning,
my soul's face will emerge,
will smile, and will begin again.

Amen.

---

*Psalm 51:10 * 2 Corinthians 5:17 * 2 Timothy 1:7*

"Create in me a clean heart, O God,
and put a new and right spirit within me."
—Psalm 51:10

When I've been running from what God's asked

Patient One,

I can be so reluctant...so resistant...
I can hear your call,
then flee in the other direction.

I can receive your vision,
then hide from its hope.

I can see your sweet grace,
then whine it's not fair.

I can stand so ready to judge those around me,
when my ground is no higher than theirs.

And, then, Patient One, you come again—
you come to my fearfulness,
arrogance, and boundary lines
with your mercy, compassion,
and steadfast love.

You come to my small vision with
an eye, a word, a touch that
can swallow the universe in love.

You come and share how forgiveness
is always an unlocked door.
What lies behind it might be unexpected,
but it promises to unbind my hurt
with welcome, strength, and affirmation.

You always give me a chance to change—
as many chances as I ask for, and more.

So, Patient One, please restore
in me some love, trust, and hope…
a clear picture of what my life might look like if
everyone were a sister and brother…
because they are.

Open my relentless grip on what I've
always known and been
that I might embrace the
callings before me here and now.

Amen.

Jonah 2:1–10 * Luke 15:20–24 * Colossians 1:13–14

"But while [the son] was still far off, his father saw him and was filled with compassion; he ran and put his arms around him and kissed him." —Luke 15:20

When I need to say thank you (even as I don't feel like it)

My Friend, my God,

In all things, I can say thank you.
Not because I am comfortable,
but because I am not alone.
And, not just companioned in this journey,
but held, loved, supported, blessed.
By You.

The One who promises
there is always, always abundance.
The One who soothingly says,
"All will be well."
The One who gives
enough light,
enough wisdom,
and enough peace
to welcome today
with vulnerability
and humble gratitude.

Your gifts come in all kinds of ways.
Please help me not to miss them.
Especially the little ones.

And, as I witness your work,
still my soul long enough to pause
and say, *Thank You.*

Amen.

*Luke 1:49 * Philippians 4:4 * 1 Thessalonians 5:18*

"Rejoice in the Lord always; again I will say, Rejoice."
—*Philippians 4:4*

When I don't want to love someone

Lord Jesus,

My very life grows from you,
the Vine from which I stem
with hope for fruit that will last.

Your love force flows through me,
and yet it also moves into
neighboring branches.

I don't want to acknowledge my
connection with some of them—
these people who block my sun
or suppress my spirit.

I struggle, Jesus, to see and
love the goodness in another,
even as your life current nourishes me
with the same sustenance.

Maybe my first step
is to simply name, each day,
our connection through you.

To remember the seed that
brought forth me also birthed them.

To unfurl my leaves—
soak in the sun, the rainfall—
and, in doing this,
open my heart to you
and *every single other*...

To keep all veins open
for transformative possibilities
that come not through my own doing,

but by being joined with you—
the One who can and does
bring redemptive relationships
I never thought possible.

Today, I will celebrate
being a part of the Vine,
and rest in the work you will do.

You only ask me to stay connected,
abiding in Love.

Amen.

*Matthew 5:7 * Luke 6:27–28 * John 15:1–11*

"I am the vine, you are the branches. Those who abide in me and I in them bear much fruit..." —John 15:5a

Prayers for
Guidance and
Transition

When I'm in the messy middle of something

Slow and Steady God,

Things have changed,
and I know they're not done changing.

I'm here on your potter's wheel
where you're shaping my essence into
something new with
guiding, loving hands.

But this messy middle time...
it's painful, and scary, and hard.
The wheel spins and my world swirls
and all I want is to see the end result.

Becoming the broken-down
lump of clay was a
hard stage too, I might add.

Help me, God,
commit to the process,
not the outcome.

Help me embrace this messy middle time
when I must make space
for shifts and questions.

Change my mantras from
clarity to exciting ambiguity,
definition to open-endedness,
certainty to awe-filled surprises,
timeline to *trust*.

Help me believe, Lord,
that even what seems
to be negative change
makes room in me and around me
for something fresh (and good).

You hum a tune of possibility
and potential as you work.
With each move of your hand,
you mutter,
"Beautiful."
"Beautiful."
"Beautiful."

And, you smile.

Amen.

*Isaiah 29:16 * Isaiah 64:8 * Jeremiah 18:1–6*

"Can I not do with you...just as this potter has done? says the LORD. Just like the clay in the potter's hand, so are you in my hand..." —Jeremiah 18:6

When I need to breathe and live into something new

Spirit of Life,

Teach me to breathe...
to gulp with desperate surrender
your life-giving energy,
not out of fear,
but because I am listening
to my primal hungers
and rejoicing in them.

The breath you give me in
this moment is a messenger,
telling me how right now
I am reborn.
I am cared for.
I am called...

Charged with the call
to channel my breath,
your life-force,
toward a gasping world.

Your breath is eternal—
never stopping,
never returning empty.

It continuously flows to
spread life and promise
if I will be a river rather than a dam.

If I listen, I will learn.

I will ride the wind of
your breath now filling me,

letting it carry me away from
my middle anchor to the
edges where I'll grow and glimpse
the purpose you have
for ever-evolving me.

Amen.

*Genesis 2:7 * 2 Corinthians 5:17 * Philippians 1:6*

"[I]f anyone is in Christ, there is a new creation:… see, every-thing has become new!" —2 Corinthians 5:17

When I need to release and receive

Dear Jesus,

Today, I release.

I release my worries.

I release the anxiety that's gnawed
a tender spot in the bottom of my soul.

I release my fear that the future's uncertain.
(Because it is, and that's okay.
You'll be with me in it.)

I release my simmering bitterness
that's bubbled on the back burner
for way...too...long.

I release my
unfair expectations
of others—
and myself, too.

I release the frustrations
and shameful secrets I've
carried under my arm for years.

I release the story or stories
I no longer want to live.

Jesus, I release.

And, today, Jesus, I receive.

I receive your love promising
I am your child,
that I am good.

I receive your peace reminding me:
*"all shall be well, and all manner
of things shall be well."*[†]

I receive your voice as the
wise whisper I follow.

I receive a new story.

Thank you, God, for receiving me—
and this whole world—
in a giant embrace,
and for receiving this prayer.

You release me to freedom
and receive all to love.

Amen.

Isaiah 43:18–19 * Ephesians 4:31—5:2 * 1 John 3:1

*"Do not remember the former things,...
I am about to do a new thing;
           now it springs forth..."
           —Isaiah 43:18a, 19a*

When I'm breaking free

Spirit of grace and grit,

You are the Giver of freedom.
I've been asking for it.
For years.
For that strength, courage,
and discipline to break free.

But, I'm now realizing
that while freedom
sometimes comes in
one, glorious breakthrough
where I burst through the
bramble into a fresh clearing,
never to turn back or tread the old path,
ready to leave the darkness
of the forest behind me...

Well, that's just not been my experience.

More often, freedom comes
through a muddy trail run where I'm
weaving and winding,
not always moving forward,
but continually progressing.

The dirt sticking to the crevices of my shoes,
the roots I knead with the soles of my feet,
the pine needles collecting in my hair,
teach me what I so wanted to leave behind
actually becomes my story.

And, how, with you,
there are no dead ends or pointless loops.
They are part of the journey...the story....
And, I need them.

When I can take in
what dim light I find
within the trees and
keep making each step
on the uneven trail,
I learn to trust.

To trust I am not lost,
but burrowed in a womb
of life-giving mystery.

And, you say,
"You are already free.
Now live into that truth."

Amen.

*Psalm 118:5 * John 8:32 * 2 Corinthians 3:17*

"[Jesus said,]... '[Y]ou will know the truth, and the truth will make you free.'" —John 8:32

When I'm not sure what to do

Wise and guiding God,

I praise you for your wisdom.
You, God, know all about me,
all about my circumstances,
all about the world around me.

You know, better than I do,
what needs to happen,
the decisions I face,
the person I'm trying to become...

But, sometimes, God, I'm paralyzed
by the choices before me.

Discernment feels like a desert,
and I'm lacking clear direction,
knowledge, and support.

I feel lost, afraid, and alone,
scorching under that hot sun
and not sure what to do.

I strain my eyes for a sign...

Are some of these images
simply mirages?

Even in my fear,
even in my frustration,
I summon thanks to you, God.

I know in time you will disperse
the clouds from my eyes,
unplug my heart,
crack open my mind,
and tune me to recognize your voice.

I believe you see what I cannot,
and your Spirit will come with
wind and water to bring me
in the direction you desire.

Please help me see what you want me to do,
then give me the courage to do what I see.

Open my eyes to those
you've placed in my life—
people exuding your loving care
in this time of seeking and searching.

I pray for your holy clarity, God,
in all my circumstances and
in the decisions I must make today.

Whatever the choice before me,
may I seek you in it.

May I choose the bigger life
with trust in my Guide...

Amen.

---

*Deuteronomy 30:19–20 * Isaiah 30:21 * Romans 12:1–2*

*"And when you turn to the right or when you turn to the left,
your ears shall hear a word behind you, saying, 'This is the
way; walk in it.'" —Isaiah 30:21*

When I don't believe what I used to

Welcoming One,

As I behold my new landscape of belief,
my expanding worldview,
my mountains of discovery and
valleys of quiet growth,
I feel—at least right now—
lonely and unmoored.

Those people, that perspective,
they used to give me belonging.
The things and voices and authorities
on which I relied are no longer here to help me.
I pendulum-swing between
judging and missing them.

I know people liked how I used to be,
and I know continuing that way would
make my life a lovely lie.

Reverting back offers no comfort.

Authenticity here and now requires
my growing, changing, and wrestling
over uncharted frontiers.
I will need companions,
and so I pray for them—
relationships of nurture
on this new path.

As I stop for respite at your wide table,
please bring, God, a whole new taste of vibrancy!

Fill my life with flavor I've yet to savor!

I want to feast on compassion and trust
the way I used to devour "certainties."
I hunger to experience your
fulfilling nourishment through
what once smelled foreign.

Your transforming table brings
a more empathetic heart,
a lens of kindness behind my eyes,
a throat burning for justice,
a commitment to the tension
I must live and love
if I am to be faithful.

When I doubt if I can be happy and alive again
in this world or in my faith,
may the thrill and freedom of your
Holy Spirit wind whoosh
through my heart and thinking,
carrying me to the Home
Who has traveled with me this whole time.

Amen.

*Psalm 139 * John 6:66–69 * Romans 8:38–39*

"Jesus asked the twelve, 'Do you also wish to go away?' Simon Peter answered him, 'Lord, to whom can we go? You have the words of eternal life.'" —John 6:67–68

When I'm wondering if this thing can live again

God, my Life and Breath,

This valley of dry bones
deadens my soul.
How could this have happened
to something so priceless?

I am staring over this
dry, lifeless pile of bones,
asking you whether it can revive...

Can you bring this back to life?
This dream?
This relationship?
This tired, sick body?
This thing into which I put so much
effort and time and sweat and skin?

Can you bring my
spirit of joy back to life?
My ability to laugh?
My ability to pray?
Can resurrection happen here
in the midst of all things
bare and brittle?
I don't really see
much potential here,
to be honest.

But, you have called me to prophesy...
to speak a message of truth
over this mess of death.

You, Lord God, are the One
who can bring me and hold me—

and all my bones—
together.

You are the One bringing
breath, life, sinews, flesh.

So, please, God, mercifully
blow toward me
some moments today
when I'll feel your breath
coursing through mine.

When I'll experience resurrection
happening in my midst,
as bones begin to rattle
and hope starts to tingle.

As I prophesy and as you breathe,
please give me, God,
the confident grace
to love what enlivens,
even if it might—or must—
look different than what died.

Ground me with patience—
patience in my prophesying
and in your promise to breathe new life.

This valley can be fertile once again.

Amen.

*Joel 2:25 * Ezekiel 37:4–6 * Luke 1:37*

"The hand of the LORD...set me down in the middle of a valley; it was full of bones... Then [God] said to me, 'Prophesy to these bones... [God] will cause breath to enter you, and you shall live." —Ezekiel 37:1, 4a, 5b

Prayers for
Waiting and
Struggle

When I need fresh faithfulness
while I wait

Strong and stable God,

I am waiting—
and I hold the waiting of
those I love.

We wait for healing,
for guidance in the big decision we're facing,
for a relationship to improve,
for the job opportunity to open,
for the person we long to marry,
for the child we crave to conceive,
for the news we ache to hear,
for the answer to our questions,
for the end to all kinds of oppression
and the rise of a world set right...

We wait—I wait—dear God, for you!
For some kind of change in my life
only you can bring.

For a shift in my foundations that
frees me to live abundantly,
differently, authentically...

I wait and do not despair
because of your goodness.

I wait and do not give up
because of your hope.

You are planting in me the seeds of
perseverance, dependence,
contentment, and trust

that will one day blossom with
a beauty beyond my imagining.

And, so, even in the bud,
in this shell of confinement,
I trust your Spirit is at work,
feeding my growth.

Keep me faithful in the waiting, dear God.

And, do not delay.

I pray in and through
the One for whom I wait.

Amen.

*Psalm 27:14 * Psalm 40:1–2 * Psalm 62:1*

"Wait for [God];
        be strong and let your heart take courage..."
                                        —Psalm 27:14

When I'm filled with frustrations and questions

God, my Rock,

You hold me fast.

You keep me steady in seasons of waiting.
You keep me trusting in seasons of struggle.
You keep me hoping in seasons of confusion.

I thank you, God, for holding me
in all these times and for
keeping all my questions...

I hear once again your call
to hold my life with open hands.
To realize I'm not as
in control as I want to be.

I plan, prepare, hope, and pray,
but, sometimes, surprises blindside me.

I try to make things go my way,
but, sometimes, they don't.

I work to change people I love,
but, sometimes, they won't.

I do my very best and work my very hardest,
but, sometimes, it's still not enough for what I want.

With your renewing fingers,
stretch and mold my spirit to
gracious nimbleness
and joyful flexibility.

Please teach me, God, to
breathe in your peace
when all seems uncertain,
and exhale anxiety
when all feels unknown.
To know it's not the end of the story
when everything feels blocked...

And, so, dear God,
I open my hands,
letting all I am and all
I hold fall into
the trustworthy hands
you stretch toward me.

Amen.

*Psalm 116:7 * Lamentations 3:21–24 * Luke 22:42*

*"But this I call to mind,
        and therefore I have hope:
The steadfast love of the LORD never ceases,
        [God's] mercies never come to an end..."
            —Lamentations 3:21–22*

When my waiting needs a shift in focus

Oh, God,

The waiting is getting long.
So long.
Too long.

I can't help but focus every day
on the thing for which I'm waiting,
or all the obstacles preventing
what I'm waiting for from happening,
or my own inability to make
what I'm waiting for happen,
or the fact it feels as if everyone
around me hasn't had to wait, but I do.

You are right.
Focusing here only increases my
feelings of hopelessness
and helplessness.

So, gracious God, patient God, trustworthy God,
please help me consider the facts,
but not make those my focus.

Keep my mind's eye and
my heart's trust on you,
the One Who has made promises—
and keeps them.

Make your presence tangibly felt
in the midst of silence and longing,
in early morning hope
and late evening tears

Thank you, God, for fueling
my endurance today.

This too will become
an occasion for strength.

Amen.

*Exodus 15:2 * Isaiah 40:29–31 * Romans 8:24–25*

*"[B]ut those who wait for the L*ORD *shall renew their strength,*
they shall mount up with wings like eagles,
they shall run and not be weary,
they shall walk and not faint."
—Isaiah 40:31

When I'm in life's winter

Enveloping God

You gather me in when
the wind of anxiety and fear whips,
when I feel my face, my heart,
tighten against the cold's force.

With wide, warm arms,
you bring me into your heart
where my angst melts by
the fire of your love.

And, it is there, as I rest and thaw,
that you remind me…

Remind me of the
unbelievable power in perseverance,
the choice to open my eyes
each morning and say,

Yes, I will keep going.
I will find grace here.
I will live from courage
instead of fear.
I will dwell in the One
Who dwells in me.

As my fears melt, dripping to my feet,
you let my real self come through…

A self you love so much…

My path toward reclamation
comes through acceptance,
through affirming I will be

gentle and forgiving toward myself
because that's how you are with me.

I will lean with all my weight
into your warmth...

My solace and strength
in life's winter.

Amen.

---

*Psalm 91:1–2 * Isaiah 25:4 * 1 Peter 5:7*

"For you have been a refuge to the poor,
*   a refuge to the needy in their distress,*
*   a shelter from the rainstorm and a shade from*
*   the heat.*
When the blast of the ruthless was like a winter rainstorm..."
*   —Isaiah 25:4*

When I feel wronged

Oh, God!

Anger is eating me alive!

My body feels steeled,
my breath stuck,
my blood simmering
over furious thought loops
that never end.
I relive the trauma of
it all with each cycle.

And, I ask you,
How can they get away with this?
Don't you see what's happening?

I feel alone and self-pitying in
my crumbling corner—
no one else knows the truth
of what's happened,
or, if they do,
they aren't helping!

Come to me, God,
like you did for Hagar—
meeting me in this wilderness
of banishment to say,
"But, *I* see you," and,
"This is not the end."

To follow and love you, God,
is to find family with those
who've endured what was far from fair.
Help me find some solidarity
and encouragement in
their pleas for justice
and tears of despair.

And, bring my eyes back to
your face, in all its
beauty and strength.

You, Jesus—you endured the
greatest injustice of all.
And, rather than defensively
fisting your hands to your face,
you stretched them out as
wide as they could go,
letting them be nailed
in one final expression of
total surrender.

You walked and led and
died with integrity even as
others lived in blindness to
what you knew.

And, in rising to life,
you proved pure love and truth
will always win in the end.

Make this fire in my belly
propel me toward obedience
I've yet to practice.

I'm handing this off to you.

Amen.

Psalm 37:7 * Isaiah 50:7-8 * Philippians 2:1–11

"Let the same mind be in you that was in Christ Jesus..."
—Philippians 2:5

When I need God to redeem this painful, hard, sad thing

Wonder Worker,

When I peered up from the hole
and saw no way out...
When what was taken
away gave no warning...
When I didn't think I
had the courage
(or even the energy)
to live into a life looking
nothing like it did before...

Something was happening.

The thing I thought would break me—
that did break me—
is now *making* me.

Great is the mystery of faith...

The pieces of life's puzzle
come together here and there,
or shockingly in a big patch at once,
and I see you...
active and good in all things.

Your power to redeem—
to take the most painful deaths
and birth from them living, breathing gifts,
taking my own breath away in awe.

You do not create pain for me to grow
or cause the heartache of my soul,
but are the expert Shaper of life's ashes.

Somehow this terrible thing—
when given in earnest to you today
(and many tomorrows from now!)—
becomes an open channel where
something amazing will flow.

A passage echoing
with a tender Voice:

You can trust me
with all the things....
in all the things...

You will lift me from this hole.

I will wail and wonder with gratitude.

I'll begin a new kind of dance,
letting my limp remind
my soul and world
how broken bodies
learn exquisite new rhythms.

With you, pain finds a home
in something larger than itself.
And, sacred scars hold haven over
wounds that will someday bless.

Amen.

---

*Genesis 45:4–8 * Joel 2:25 * 2 Corinthians 4:16–18*

"So we do not lose heart. Even though our outer nature is
wasting away, our inner nature is being renewed day by day.
For this slight momentary affliction is preparing us for an
eternal weight of glory beyond all measure..."
—2 Corinthians 4:16–17

When I cry for the world

Merciful Jesus,

I cry for our world.
I cry over broken bodies
and broken homes
and broken hearts.

I cry over violence
and exclusion
and indifference.

I cry most of all over the children!

Through my body and breath,
I pray for your kin-dom...

For all to have
nourishing food and nurturing homes,
edifying work and safe, skilled schools,
compassionate healthcare and dignified wages,
soft beds to fall into at the day's close...

For the children to be protected,
the elderly honored,
and both hugged every single day...

For reparative justice,
cherished diversity,
and peaceful purity in what's
breathed, eaten, and drunk.

I cry and I pray,
confessing the many times
I've declared what I deserve
rather than asked what I could give.

I cry and I pray,
knowing I'm complicit in the pain
and essential to the healing.

I cry and I pray,
trusting my tears mingle with your own,
hoping this tearful river softens and shapes
the hardest canyons of injustice—
or at least lays the groundwork.

I pray and I act,
moving my body and resources
toward your kin-dom vision,
trusting my skills and gifts
carry forward the new, just world you imagine
and are always bringing.

I remember this work is mine to do.

"Christ has no body but yours,
No hands, no feet on earth but yours,
Yours are the eyes with which he looks
Compassion on this world,
Yours are the feet with which
he walks to do good,
Yours are the hands, with which
he blesses all the world..."[†]

O Jesus, have mercy
and help me.

Amen.

*Isaiah 58:6–12 * Lamentations 2:19 * Luke 4:18–19*

"The Spirit of the Lord is upon me,
    because the Lord has anointed me
        to bring good news to the poor.
[The Spirit] has sent me to proclaim release to the captives
    and recovery of sight to the blind,
        to let the oppressed go free..."
            —Luke 4:18

Prayers for
Trust

When I'm surprised, scared, and need to surrender

Spirit of surprise
and faithfulness,

When I encounter change
I did not choose...

When life feels
out of control (my control!),
unpredictable,
scary...

When my normal coping mechanisms
aren't available this time around...

When the overarching question is,
What do I do now?

Your reassuring, Spirit-filled wind
comes blowing at my back,
announcing I'm not alone,
that you will fill me with everything
I need to take on what's next
and do the things I didn't think possible.

You are the master Improviser,
and I will learn from my Teacher.

This is how you do it...
yes and yes and yes and yes...

Help me ride
the current of this
Pentecostal wind.

Use this change in plans
to be a change in heart,
that I might not move
forward with a dead soul,
clinging to what's known,
yet no longer there.

Open my heart to what you will do in
this pocket of open space between
before and after
(even if this involves a lot
of blowing around and burning).

Today,
I say yes
and yes
and yes
and yes...

Amen.

*Ruth 1:1–22 * Psalm 104:4 * Acts 2:1–5*

*"[S]uddenly from heaven there came a sound like the rush of
a violent wind... All of them were filled with the Holy Spirit..."
—Acts 2:2a, 4a*

When I need to trust where I am is right

Reassuring One,

Today, with your help,
I will release my ruminating...

Today, with your help,
I will welcome what is—
not in resignation, but in trust.
Life won't always be this way.
And, maybe, just maybe, I need this
in order to get where I'm going.

Today, I will thank you
for the value imbedded
in my work and time.

Today, rather than taking consensus
from everything and
everyone around me
about what I need to do,
I will stop.

I will let myself be in
that uncomfortable quiet.

I will do my deepest listening
for the most important Voice
whose tone is pure silence
and who likes to stay small.

I can choose these things today, God,
because these are your promises—
to handle what I can't,
to use what I'd rather not endure,

to give me the inner wisdom
I need for each choice.

So I say thanks, praise, and okay.

Amen.

---

*1 Kings 19:11–13 * Psalm 4:4 * Psalm 46:10*

"Be still, and know that I am God!"
          —Psalm 46:10a

When I need to trust there's enough time

Dear Jesus,

You tell me to consider "lilies" and "birds."
You promise me "I have everything I need."
You call me to surrender in trust.
You sing me into greater slowness,
where I can believe there
is somehow enough time.
That I am enough.

I clutch onto the
crazies and the frantic.
The spin of so much activity
makes me feel productive.
Productivity means success,
means value, means admiration;
is...lie.

Belovedness as your child
means good, means enough, means yes;
is...Truth.

This is my identity,
never lost and never earned.
I keep thinking I must work
for what I've had the whole time.

I can never live as you call me to, Jesus,
when I am hurried and scattered,
swinging from item to item on
that scrap of bullet-pointed scribble
gloating on the counter.

Even when I do every
item on that list,

it doesn't mean I come to
the end of the day satisfied,
or that I go to bed with
a heartbeat of peace.

What is true in my fritter of activity
proves true in my prayers.
I so swiftly swipe away the
sweetness of one answered prayer
because I've already focused
on the next need.

Like a cloud, my anxiety shifts,
hovering from one corner
of life's landscape to the next.

But, for today—
and maybe I'll only make it today—
I trust there is enough time to
do and be that for which you ask.

I will melt into the resting ground
of green pastures and still waters
where the frenzy cannot reach.

I will use what time I have
to make it a resting ground for
all your children.

Amen.

*Deuteronomy 33:12 * Psalm 23:2–3 * Matthew 6:26–30*

*"Consider the lilies of the field, how they grow; they neither
toil nor spin... [I]f God so clothes the grass of the field...will
[God] not much more clothe you...?" —Matthew 6:28b, 30*

When I need to know I'm held (just as I am!)

Gracious God,

Please meet me where I'm at today.

Enfold my heart—
whatever its state—
reminding me you are here,
reminding me I am loved.

I thank you, God,
I don't need to be perfect.
Your grace is deeper,
your love stronger,
your forgiveness broader
than I understand.

Draw me out, Lord.
Shine your light on my secrets.
Send the soft rains of cleansing and
the strong rains of refinement
on my soul's ground.

Please prepare me
for the days ahead,
whatever they bring.

You've given me the Spirit to face it all.

I hand over my worries and joys,
knowing you care even
more deeply than I do.

Please make me an instrument
of your love today, God.

Make me a reflection of my Creator
in what I say,
in how I act,
in the focus of my thoughts,
in the energy I emanate.

Amen.

Psalm 51:2 * 2 Corinthians 3:18 * Ephesians 3:18–19

"I pray that you…know the love of Christ that surpasses knowledge, so that you may be filled with all the fullness of God." —Ephesians 3:18a, 19

When I need some holy memory

Faithful God,

Like a tree holding
sacred stories within its trunk,
I began and now breathe
because of dark, damp earth.

Gazing back on my life,
I'm freshly amazed at how
you've worked before…
surprises and fidelity
intrinsic to the
person I now am.

Memories of deliverance
ground me once again
as the wind around
me picks up.

I dig with hopeful courage,
intertwining my soul with
your anchoring roots—
praising you as my Protector,
leaning on your wisdom,
soaking in your love,
seeking you for daily
strength and stability.

I need those memories, God,
as I weather new storms—
major changes, struggles,
frustrations, and anger…
ripping limbs off,
leaving me stark and bare.

Yet in each year's mercies,
a ring grows within my trunk—
some rings thick from lush seasons,
some thin and light from drought.

I continue to grow and become,
all through your grace
keeping my roots in
dark dampness
that keeps me alive.

Amen.

*Deuteronomy 5:15 * Psalm 1:1–3 * Psalm 77:11–20 **

"I will call to mind the deeds of the LORD;
I will remember your wonders of old."
—Psalm 77:11

When I don't feel ready for this

Lord Jesus,

I'm finding kinship with your disciples...
soul friends who followed you immediately
when you met them
in boats tangled with fishing nets
or on stone walls near wells
or counting the clink of tax money.

These siblings of mine who
were willing to follow your lead
when they didn't feel ready...

Rather than sitting down to reason,
they stood up to respond,
and chose every morning
to move their feet,
even as their minds questioned
and their hearts worried.

Can I do that today?
With your help?
With theirs?

You tell me an element of fear
always accompanies the most
worthwhile ventures.

And, I feel in my body
the age-old wisdom—
if I wait 'til I'm ready,
I'll eternally wait.

If I block potential pain,
I also thwart what could be
my life's greatest joy.

I pray that, even in my confusion,
I can be committed—
asking you all my questions
while we continue to walk.

Amen.

---

*Matthew 4:18–22 * Matthew 9:9 * John 4:27–30*

"And [Jesus] said to them, 'Follow me, and I will make you fish for people.' Immediately they left their nets and followed him." —Matthew 4:19–20

When I'm unsure and doubting

One Who knows me best,

There are times I sense
more clearly your direction,
confident in what I need to do.
Those are the times I feel
stable...steady...focused.

But, more often, Lord,
I'm in that inner fog where
the call and light are faint.
I struggle to remember if
I heard your voice at all,
and the cacophony of questions
becomes the tolling bell I hear—
each ring another round of

Are you sure?
Did God really say...
Turn around!
You're alone.

It's in this time
I trust what (and Who)
initiated in me this
path in the first place.
I remember that you, Jesus,
were countlessly asked if you trusted,
proving again and again
how you did.

Every day is practice to trust again—
sometimes, like Samuel,
I will need many tries
before recognizing your word.

And, some days, I will need to listen for
echoes of your voice in my heart
amid the silence in my ears.

Please keep speaking,
and reminding,
and holding me fast.
I will do my best to
settle my heart
and perk my ears for my
best listening and availability...

"Tis so sweet to trust in Jesus,
Just to take Him at His Word;
Just to rest upon His promise,
Just to know, 'Thus saith the Lord!'

"Jesus, Jesus, how I trust Him!
How I've proved Him o'er and o'er;
Jesus, Jesus, precious Jesus!
Oh, for grace to trust Him more!

"Yes, 'tis sweet to trust in Jesus,
Just from sin and self to cease;
Just from Jesus simply taking
Life and rest, and joy and peace."[†]

Amen.

Genesis 3:1 * 1 Samuel 3:1–11 * Matthew 4:1–11

"Speak, Lord, for your servant is listening." —1 Samuel 3:9

When I claim belief beyond what I see

Sweet Provider,

You course as the ongoing Source,
the life-giving Current,
the Stream flowing beneath me at all times.

You move under every step I take,
nourishing my path (and me) with
what is most valuable and could
never be measured.

I hear your water's gurgling song,
a melody of continual abundance
from the self-replenishing spring.
You freely give what is always generating.

There is more here than meets my eyes,
and just because I don't see it now
doesn't mean it isn't there.

You never lead me to a place
without what I need.
What can I do but keep walking forward,
humble and reflective,
remembering what you've done before?

With joy, I will draw and drink,
readying myself for the
miracles ahead.

Amen.

*Isaiah 12:3–4 * John 7:37–38 * Hebrews 11:1*

"Out of the believer's heart shall flow rivers of living water."
—John 7:38b

When I need to do something scary

O God,

I know I need to take
this courageous next step,
but the vulnerability paralyzes me.

The status quo is unsustainable,
yet I grasp for its hollow promises of
safety and stability.

If I don't do the thing I know I must,
my soul will shrivel.

But if I do?

Thick insecurities cloak me, God,
with questions I'm afraid to answer:

Who am I to think I can do this?
Who am I to speak up and out?
Who am I to say you've directed me
out of the boat and onto these waves?

My fear of others thwarts me, God,
with sinister scoffs and prickly judgment.

What if they don't believe me?
What if they judge me?
What if they think I'm ridiculous,
or arrogant, or selfish?

What if I fail?
What if I'm a fool?

Fatalism is my forte.

You promise, God, you're the Great I AM —
the One who will be with me
as I face this scary step,
and the next one after that.

You'll patiently prod
as I relentlessly doubt.
You're simply inviting me
to say yes to this first step.

Dissipate the power of
my *"who am I's"* as I hear your voice,
my *"what if they's"* as I see your face,
my *"what if I's"* as I feel your hand.

Make my feet follow my breath, God—
exhaling what was needed before,
inhaling what's asked of me now.

Keep me walking forward,
courageous albeit shaky.
Give me trust and faithfulness
as my guardrails.

Here we go.

Amen.

*Exodus 4:10–20 * Esther 4:9–17 * Matthew 14:22–33*

"Take heart, it is I; do not be afraid." —Matthew 14:27b

Prayers for
Comfort and
Strength

When I ache with hurt

Spirit who groans with
sighs too deep for words,

I lean into and rest in those sighs.
I find in your pleas and
petitions a home for
my ache,
my dismay,
and so much anger.

I hold your hand as you
help me sift through
each layer of betrayal,
my feelings of being deceived,
my temptation to turn against—
to blame, to ignore, to lose sight
of the "you" within others,
however deeply buried.

You've told me you cannot heal
what I don't give space to grieve and feel.
And, so, I trust that no
feeling is final or forever.
That there is room and
respect and honor
for tears and incredulity
and deep, deep sadness.

So, Holy Spirit, would you meld
my sighs and groans into your own,
bringing me into a love
for you above all else?

Would you make firm the weak knees
and quench the parched voice,
that I might serve your communion,
overflowing with peace and healing?

Would you stretch my fingertips
to the wounds of the breaking,
tenderly showing them
how wide your arms are?

And, would you ignite in me
bravery to live the gospel
with new passion and intensity?

I give you thanks for your embrace
of all I can pray and all I cannot.

And that this can be enough.

In the love and grace
of my wounded Healer...

Amen.

---

*Psalm 25:15–17 * Isaiah 35:3 * Romans 8:26 **

"The Spirit helps us in our weakness;...interced[ing] with sighs too deep for words." —Romans 8:26

When I need to rest in grace

Today, Merciful God,
I lay down my private,
clenched-hands salvation projects.

I fall, arms wide, eyes open,
into your ocean of grace...

All because you are
trustworthy in what you say,
faithful in what you do,
loving in how you respond,
patient in what you ask.

You've taught me how
to take in the struggle...
to look at it,
hold it in my hands,
allow it to teach me,
and let it lead me
toward a new place
of delightful dependence on you.

A gorgeous, expansive place of
release, joy, and trust.

You're showing me it's not who I *am*
that's keeping me from you
and what you desire,
but who I keep saying I'm *not*.

At least today,
I let go of who I am
that I might be stretched
into what I must become.

I'll ride the waves,
knowing grace upon grace
promises good land ahead.

In the love of the Great Surfer...

Amen.

*John 1:16 * Romans 6:14 * Ephesians 2:8*

"For by grace you have been saved through faith, and this is not your own doing; it is the gift of God..." —Ephesians 2:8

When I long for healing

Dearest Jesus,

You devoted yourself to healing.
I praise and thank you for
the sight you restored,
the souls you freed,
the broken legs you made to run,
the flaking skin you smoothed with love.

I praise you for the
homeless hearts you gave a resting place,
the insecure identities you brought purpose,
the torn relationships you offered restoration,
the lives plagued by evil you freed once and for all.

You opened your arms to
broken people, Lord, and said,
Come to me...

And, so, Jesus, I come to you.

I need help from beyond myself,
and I reach toward you for
healing and wholeness.

I know you are willing
to enter my pain,
my fear,
my anxiety,
my doubt, confusion,
exhaustion, and desperation.

Please renew my trust, Lord Christ.
I know being honest and crying out to you
opens the path toward deeper healing.

I may not be cured,
but, in you, I can be whole.

I hang my prayers on you, asking, trusting,
that your consolation will come.

How gracious you are to me.

Today, I claim your healing
and ask that a fresh perseverance
take hold in my life.

Amen.

*Matthew 11:28–30 * Mark 5:25–34 * Luke 8:49–55*

"Come to me, all you that are weary and are carrying heavy burdens, and I will give you rest." —Matthew 11:28

When I'm grieving a goodbye

Compassionate One,

Be with me in my goodbyes.

When I'm asked to
open my hands and
release what I've held—
held *tightly*—
place your peace
between the fingers.

Put your comfort in
the cracks and crevices
of my heart.

Use my falling tears
as nourishment for
this ground of grief,
bearing fruit for
a new season
also promising sweetness.

Amen.

*Matthew 5:4 * John 12:24 * Revelation 21:3–5*

"[U]nless a grain of wheat falls into the earth and dies, it remains just a single grain; but if it dies, it bears much fruit."
—John 12:24

When I have a hole of loss in my heart

Comforting God,

You know my empty spaces.
You find the gaping holes of loss
and bury yourself *right there*.

You make a home in
my broken heart
and go about the
work you do best,
which is healing...
which is hope-creating...
which is resurrection.

You do not make
the hole go away.

No, you honor the hole.

The hole is precious,
because that hole was
something important to me...
a person, a relationship, a dream,
a season of life to which
I'll never return.

But, you whisper there are
things you can do
in and through that
hole I now have;
that sometimes spaces
form the perfect place
for beauty to birth and emerge.

So, in this moment, God, I let my
holes be known and ask
you to do that healing,
hope-creating,
resurrection-filled
work in them.

You are my restoration.

Amen.

*Psalm 119:50 * Isaiah 66:13 * 2 Corinthians 1:3–5*

*"Blessed be the...God of all consolation, who consoles us in
all our affliction, so that we may be able to console those
who are in any affliction with the consolation with which we
ourselves are consoled by God." —2 Corinthians 1:3–4*

When my body's in pain

Tender Holder of my
hurting body and tired heart,

I still and settle my soul
in your hands,
giving to you
the places of pain,
asking you to channel
your breath through mine,
bringing balm and comfort—
even for a moment.

You softly tend with
a soothing Spirit the
sharp spikes of pain
spearing their way
with suddenness and
stealing my breath for a second.

You don't abandon me
to face my limitations.
You are teaching me
to lean into them,
and find there a
whole new depth of
sustaining grace.

I can rest in the
cradling of your love
while together we wait
for muscles to mend,
bones to solidify,
and disease to die.

You will renew my
heart every morning with
strength to love my body
even as it feels an enemy.
This, too, will pass....

And, that is sufficient hope
to get me through today.

Amen.

Psalm 147:3 * Isaiah 43:1–7 * Colossians 1:11–12

"When you pass through the waters, I will be with you;
*   and through the rivers, they shall not overwhelm you;*
when you walk through fire you shall not be burned,
*   and the flame shall not consume you."*
                                        —Isaiah 43:2

When I need to remember
I'm an overcomer

Strong and Loving God,

In you,
through you,
because of you,
I am an overcomer.

Thank you for helping me trust amid setbacks…
for training me to see how progress
isn't a straight line, but a squiggly one
marked by moments when I put my hands on
my knees and gasp for breath.

I keep my eyes forward
that I might see the
promise before me.

Through my sweat today,
I'm building new strength
and skill for tomorrow.

The simple choice to try again,
to show up and do the work,
is victory in your book.

Help me find a goal that's attainable for now,
and, tomorrow, one a little further down the road.

I will be less overwhelmed that way…

And, that's how you do it—
sneaking me into believing
I can do this thing.

Yours is the coaching
voice I need most,
speaking directly in
my ear as you run alongside,
stride for stride:

I believe in you.
I am with you.
We will overcome
this together.

Amen.

Psalm 121 * 2 Timothy 4:7–8 * Hebrews 12:1–2

"Let us run with perseverance the race that is set before us,
looking to Jesus..." —Hebrews 12:1b–2a

When I'm longing for peace,
within and without

Beautiful Spirit of Peace,

I am longing for peace within
and peace around...

For peace in families,
peace in neighborhoods,
peace between nations,
peace for mother earth,
peace in the quiet depths
of my own soul.

Peace for people ripped open
by painful divides on
streets and in conversations...

Peace for friends facing
suicide or prison...

Peace for loved ones living through
divorce and death and hard anniversaries...

Peace for people leaving home
because their job relocated
or the money wasn't there anymore...

Peace for those who uncovered a shocking
revelation about someone they loved,
and they aren't sure what to do or whom to trust.

Peace for all whose
greatest fears actualized
before their eyes,
and sighs and tears
became a daily language.

Peace that holds all of
us in wholeness
when we're carrying
grief or heartache,
chaos or tumultuous questions.

When what's most precious to us
was swept away in one swift wave,
or the world's teeming with
so much noise and busyness
we can't hear ourselves think.

I ask you, Spirit of peace and hope,
to blow a breath of balm upon the wounds,
and lead us toward bone-deep belief.

Even in this challenging landscape,
may your presence bring
peace passing all understanding
as it strengthens bodies,
renews minds,
and heals this land.

I thank you that peace is not a dream,
but a promise.

And you are the Giver of Peace.

Amen.

---

*Matthew 5:9 * Luke 1:28–32 * John 14:27*

*"[Jesus said,] 'Peace I leave with you; my peace I give to you...
Do not let your hearts be troubled, and do not
let them be afraid.'" —John 14:27*

When I need to pour out my heart

Good Shepherd,

You see a path when I only see roadblocks.
You keep hope when I'm at the bottom of my reserve.
You provide strength when every muscle—
physical, spiritual, emotional (need I go on?)—
burns with fatigue.
You fiercely protect me when
all forms of attack
sneak up on my shoulder.

So, I pour my heart out before you,
asking you to gently take and tend
the troubles that feel relentless...
the joys I pray will last...
the longings embedded so deeply within
that every breath aches for their fulfillment...

I will keep coming to you,
lying down on this
bit of pasture or temple floor—
the place my knees, lips, and heart
rest on holy ground you've cleared just for me.

I pour out my heart and soul, Loving Lord,
knowing you hear in your mercy
and respond in your grace.
I will settle into the arms of my Shepherd.

Amen.

---

*Psalm 62:8 * Isaiah 40:11 * John 10:11*

"Trust in [God] at all times, O people;
pour out your heart before [God];
God is a refuge for us.
—Psalm 62:8

When I feel as if I can't go on

Sustainer of my broken body
and despondent spirit,

When I feel overwhelmed and want to hide,
when I feel trapped and want to escape,
when the tears of dependence
and fear wash me over...

I come back to today, today, today.

I open needy hands
for daily manna.
I look for joy in *this*
because of what you
might build in me.

And, I scrawl some more on my ever-growing list
of your faithfulness in the path toward growth.

My heart can sing, can cry,
can hold the linking arms of faith and hope
through this crucible of transformation.

Use it for good, God.
Use it for good.

Amen.

---

*Romans 8:28 * 2 Corinthians 4:8 * Philippians 1:6*

*"We know that all things work together for good for those
who love God, who are called according to [God's] purpose."
—Romans 8:28*

When I can't sleep

Quieting God,

I ask for your gentle strength to
cover my fears tonight.
I'm afraid of the darkness,
afraid of the uncontrollable,
afraid of the unthinkable.

I'm afraid of tomorrow.
How will I make it through the day?
How will I care for people who depend on me?
How will I perform to meet expectations
when I cannot think clearly
(or fall asleep on the job)?

I despair I will never sleep again,
caught in the fear coiling around my heart
and anxiety compressing my mind.

I ask, Soothing One,
that your presence
would fill me with holy calm.
That you would lift this pressure
and deepen my breathing.

I ask that your Spirit of peace
would whisper your truth in my ears,
reminding me I need not be afraid.
The fears feel so convincing and so real....
in my heart and in this world.

Though the fears may not dissipate,
your assurance strengthens me to face them.
To name them for the small things they are
in comparison to the Great One within me.

Regardless of how I feel come morning,
you will not leave me to face the day alone.

For the simple acts of living and loving,
of sleeping and trusting,
I need your holy comfort, God.

I will feel my body sink into this bed
as my heart sighs into your hands.

All will be well.

Amen.

---

*Psalm 4:8 * Luke 12:32 * 1 John 4:4*

*"I will both lie down and sleep in peace;
       for you alone, O Lord, make me lie down in safety."*
                              —Psalm 4:8

Prayers for
Seasonal and
Liturgical Times

For the New Year

Gracious One,

I thank you for holding my
hand in this fresh, new year...
Against my inclination
and with your help,
I let go of my desire for
more control over my life.

My hunger to know what's coming
and to be ready for it.

My expectations to be in charge.

Have you not taught me again and again
how the joy is in the flexibility?
How all the unexpected,
the unwanted, the unexplained
things coalesce to carve me into
the person I really want to be?

Even the changes I asked for,
the changes I wanted,
can cause anxiety.

Treading on this shifting soil
calls for a steadiness
beyond my own capabilities.

So, I trust your hand to hold mine,
carrying me into this new land—
good but different.

You are my Birthing Mother,
always re-creating,
always open to change.

You keep showing me
while change is eternally constant,
so is your presence.

You engrain in me
how hope is born through struggle
and the fresh start brought through
change is an invitation to grow.

Whenever something leaves,
something new comes.

Please give me the
wisdom of soul, Loving One,
to look for it.

For, a soft heart open to newness,
sensitive to others' pain,
resilient with hope,
trusting in darkness...
this is the heart for
which I pray this year.

Amen.

---

*Jeremiah 29:11 * Ezekiel 11:9 * 1 Corinthians 2:9*

"[N]o eye has seen, nor ear heard,
          nor the human heart conceived,
what God has prepared for those who love [God]..."
          —1 Corinthians 2:9

For Valentine's Day

Loving God,

As I think about Valentine's Day,
I bring you my heart...
a hopeful heart,
a disappointed heart,
a confident heart,
a heart in hiding,
a grateful heart,
an angry heart,
a patient or "I'm so done and over with this" heart,
a restless heart,
a full or aching-with-hollowness heart,
a scarred heart,
a scared heart,
a heart that sings or
a heart long silent,
a surprised heart,
a struggling heart,
a broken heart,
a beautiful heart...

I wear my heart as the badge of honor it is—
any heart that keeps beating love
in a broken world
is a testimony to grace,
to resurrection,
to you...

Somehow, God, you find a way to curl yourself
into the most-closed hearts...
to make your way through
the heart's minefield,
knowing where to step,
where to heal.

I know, God, that broken,
beautiful hearts are powerful—
the world was changed, is changed,
because of your broken, beautiful heart.

And, there's beauty to be found in the pieces...

Thank you God—
Love made Flesh—
for hiding me in your heart.

Amen.

Mark 12:30–31 * John 1:14 * Ephesians 3:16–17

*"[L]ove the Lord your God with all your heart, and with
all your soul, and with all your mind, and with all your
strength." —Mark 12:30*

For Lent

Redeeming One,

You came, Jesus, to show me the
best way to live and walk this path.

You let yourself feel the depth
of need surrounding you.
You kept a purity of focus.
You always, always chose love.

All with bravery and trust.

I need you, Jesus, to walk
beside me now,
helping me reflect,
confess, prepare...

This Lenten path puts before me
the questions and realizations
I so often stuff away.

With each step, I'm recognizing
barriers built through my
rote habits and unrealized prejudices,
my baseline grudges and routine neglects...
I must acknowledge compromises
that drew me further away
from my own soul and your calling.

But, I'm coming back home.

Hone my desires to that
pure focus you held.

Help me fast from self-absorption,
finding my sustenance in the
rich profundity of suffering-love.

Draw my heart and feet forward
on this path that's both total mystery
and innate to who I am in you.

A minor melody marks our cadence,
yet you tune my ears for more than that.
Resurrection is always the final number.

Help me walk, Savior Lord,
with hope amid heaviness,
ears to the ground.

I will welcome my mortality
and the potential in ashes and dust.

Amen.

*Psalm 51:17 * Isaiah 53:4–6 * Luke 9:23–24*

"If any want to become my followers, let them deny themselves and take up their cross daily and follow me."
—Luke 9:23

For Springtime

Loving, Creator God,

Spring reminds me it's
never too late to start over.
That there's been quiet growth
over these long months
of winter when I saw nothing.
When I was called to believe
there was growth happening
beneath hard, cold soil.

And now? Glory!

I celebrate the loveliness
of all you've made.
The newness, Lord,
the freshness—
it inspires my soul!

Tulips in the front yard,
buds on the trees,
the voices of birds,
the cleansing of rain,
the comfort of sunshine...
Each gift renews me,
speaking of the promise within
all those months of dormancy
and preparation.

As spring awakens my physical senses,
I ask, God, for you to awaken my inner senses.

May my mind open and blossom
to the longings you've placed within me...
to the steps and path that will
satisfy the desires of my heart...

to the hopes and passions
you've planted in every
one of your children...

May I seek what will truly fulfill them.
May I journey toward their Source.
May I be guided by your gentle and wise Spirit.

It is never too late to be
what you call me to be.
Even as it takes greatest courage
and deepest humility.

With your help, I will open myself to
what I never expected before,
never experienced before,
and never thought possible.

Amen.

*Psalm 16:11 * Psalm 104:24–30 * Isaiah 55:8–9*

"You show me the path of life.
In your presence there is fullness of joy..."
—Psalm 16:11a

For Summer's ending

Near One,

Thank you for all the ways you've
companioned me this summer.

You've traveled with me as I
made road trips to visit scattered, special family,
waited at airport gates thick with frustrating delays,
buckled kids in the car for an adventure at the zoo,
driven across town to eat
crisp cold salads with a dear friend,
folded clothes and packed the suitcase another time.

You've traveled with me, Jesus,
as I've sat in medical waiting rooms,
as I've kissed loved ones goodbye while holding back tears,
as I've lingered by the window with a cup of coffee,
overcome with too many thoughts to name...

You've made your presence known
through tracked-in sand on the kitchen floor
and the smell of fresh strawberries dumped on the counter.

I've heard your voice in the
joyful shrieks of children in sprinklers
and the creak of the porch swing as dusk settled.

You've held me through weeks that were stressful
and weeks that evaporated in elation...
weeks when I was complacent and selfish
and weeks I was sacrificial and servant-hearted...
weeks when I was honest and integrated
and weeks I didn't even recognize
the person in the mirror....

You never failed to remind me
how you loved me and still
had good for me to do.

Sometimes I caught your message...

How I thank you,
traveling and strengthening One,
for going with me through these summer months...
for offering reassurance as I enter
the fall and all its change.

I hold out my gratitude for what was
and my quiet hopes for what's to come.

Amen.

Genesis 46:4 * Deuteronomy 31:8 * Psalm 139:7–10 *

"Where can I go from your spirit?
    Or where can I flee from your presence?...
If I take the wings of the morning
        and settle at the farthest limits of the sea,
even there your hand shall lead me,
        and your right hand shall hold me fast."
                    —Psalm 139:7, 9–10

For Autumn

Gracious God,

I praise you as the
Giver and Renewer of seasons.
The earth's rhythms
remind me of
your faithfulness…
your love…
your promises…

The sun rising each morning,
the leaves turning and dropping,
the stars peeking through
mists of morning gray,
then greeting me as
the day kisses night.

Amidst the cycle, I find
a rhythm for my soul.
I hear echoes of that
ancient and eternal place
into which you beckon me,
and I say thank you.

Oh, God, how will you
show yourself to me today?

I am longing for
a closer connection,
a stronger fire,
a self-forgetting confidence
that fills me and makes me
a whole, abundant person.

I want to find myself so full
of your loving presence

that it spills and splashes
over my life's rim,
blessing and baptizing
every trip I make,
every meal I cook,
every task I do,
every person I meet,
every smile I share,
every worry I carry.

Thank you, God, for lifting me
over the threshold of this season.

May I watch for the stars tonight
and the sun tomorrow,
finding you in both.

Amen.

Psalm 19:1–6 * Galatians 2:20 * Colossians 3:17

"The heavens are telling the glory of God;
and the firmament proclaims God's handiwork."
—Psalm 19:1

For All Saints' Day

God of welcome and warmth,

I'm a bit melancholy—
or maybe it's pensive—
in approaching this All Saints' Day.

It's a beautiful day—
this time to remember and give thanks
for the saints who have graced my life.
These angels—
raw, real, and devoted
in their humanity—
who have encouraged me,
emboldened me,
taught me what I needed
to know to survive…

I think of parents, grandparents,
partners, wives, husbands,
sisters, brothers,
teachers, colleagues,
neighbors, friends—
some of them did seem
pretty unlikely characters
to be your saints,
but the more I live,
the more I realize
that's pretty typical of you
and your choosing.

I am grateful for these
quirky, lovely individuals
who have gone before me, but
whose light still shines,
bringing warmth and illumination
to my own journey.

Their whispers of wisdom
help me hunger for a deeper
wholeness found in you.

They tell me I can be a saint too...

You have called me, like those before me,
to do things with a great, tidal love,
covering the ache of this world.
So, I answer this calling, God, with all I am.
I bring you myself and my prayers
for all those on my heart.

I thank you, God, for the
saints of then and
the saints of now...
for the saint you are
kindling inside of me.

May I remain grateful for their impact
on my life and heart—
the truth they spoke and lived,
the faith they held and passed on,
the love they modeled and shared.

Amen.

*Jeremiah 1:5 * Hebrews 11:1—12:2 * 2 Timothy 1:5–7*

*"Since we are surrounded by so great a cloud of witnesses,...
let us run with perseverance the race that is set before us..."*
—Hebrews 12:1

A parent's Advent prayer

Dear God,

I now stop what I'm doing,
what I'm thinking,
what I'm scrambling to plan
and hustling to finish
so that I can
be here.

Be here in the safety and warmth of your love.
This love that holds me fast and keeps me centered.

What I want to be a season of joy for my children
so quickly becomes a season of
increased expectations for me—
not because *they* expect things,
but because I do.

It's the pressure I put on myself to
make things perfect,
and memorable,
and happy,
and "special."

But, you came to me amidst darkness and stars—
reminding me how darkness and light
are most beautiful together.
And, in that holy, mysterious and messy night,
you redefined perfection,
promising me that leaning into the mystery
and laying down in loving awe
compose the most faithful response.

You tell me the best gift I can give
my children this Christmas is
to look with love into their eyes.

To pause throughout the day
to pray over them.

To envelop them with arms
of fierce grace when I feel
most angry or annoyed.

To sit in wonder for a moment (or many)
and marvel at all that shaped
our family this year.

To give thanks
and allow tears to fall
and dreams to rise.

To take my pilgrim band
by their hands and walk together,
deep into the heart of Bethlehem
shining bright within our souls.

This will be more than enough,
because you've made a manger
in which my heart will rest and find
your heartbeat becoming mine.

Amen.

---

*Matthew 2:10–11 * Matthew 6:31 * Luke 2:15–20*

*"Let us go now to Bethlehem and see this thing that has
taken place, which the Lord has made known to us."*
—Luke 2:15b

For Christmas Day

Lord Jesus,

You've asked me to be a womb
for you this Advent—
to be a space where your
love grows and your grace expands.

You've asked me to let the sides of my soul stretch
that I might become large with your promise.
Being a womb for you has pushed me
to the furthest rim of who I am.

You've asked me to grow for
people who never say "thank you"
(or "I'm sorry").

You've called me to care for children
who pull me to new levels
of selflessness.

You've softened my gritted teeth
in tough phone calls
or repetitive criticism,
all while my soul
groaned with growth.

In the pain, you enlarged me.
In the swelling, you dwelt within me.

And, when I questioned whether I could
make any more room in myself or my life for you—
the One who asks everything of me—
your Spirit brought me forward
in its quiet, miraculous way.

You whispered my hollowing
was for a yet greater filling.

And now today, Lord Jesus,
you are born.
Born in me,
born to me,
born for me.
Thank you, Lord Jesus,
Immanuel.

Amen.[†]

Luke 1:38 * Luke 2:10–14 * Galatians 2:20

"Then Mary said, 'Here am I, the servant of the Lord; let it be
with me according to your word.'" —Luke 1:38

A blessing for someone you love (and yourself!)

Loving God,

I pray for your love in _____'s life.
I pray for your joy in _____'s heart.
I pray for your peace in _____'s soul.
I pray for your patience in _____'s words.
I pray for your kindness in _____'s actions.
I pray for your goodness in _____'s sharing.
I pray for your faithfulness in _____'s relationships.
I pray for your gentleness in _____'s spirit.
And, I pray for your self-control in _____'s choices.

Love, joy, peace, patience, kindness,
goodness, faithfulness, gentleness, and self-control.
May they blossom in and through_____.

Amen.

---

*Numbers 6:26 * Isaiah 11:2–3 * Galatians 5:22–23*

"The fruit of the Spirit is love, joy, peace, patience, kindness, generosity, faithfulness, gentleness, and self-control."
—Galatians 5:22–23a

Closing Thoughts

From Dr. Tom Braithwaite (1956–2014)

One of my most powerful teachers about the pilgrim's prayerful journey was my father. In recent years, I uncovered an email he'd sent me during his long sojourn with cancer and before his death in 2014. His pilgrimage was in and of itself a beautiful prayer—one that would later birth *Ash and Starlight* for me.

* * *

February 24, 2011

Dear Arianne,

It is tempting, for all of us, to measure God's blessing in some type of tangible way, looking at the "good gifts" as signs of His love and favor, and to "answered prayers" as evidence that God really is listening and that we somehow changed His mind in mid-stream. I don't think that takes into serious account the nature of God's sovereignty, nor the substance of prayer.

It is also easier for those who subscribe to the so-called "success theology" to lean into interpretations of life events in such a superficial way. Anyone who truly plumbs the depths of suffering and evil in this world does not find such answers satisfactory for very long. Given these past eight years, I have mused on such things quite a bit.

God truly makes the rain fall upon the just and the unjust. The thorn is not always removed. The cup not only doesn't pass us by, it smacks us in the face. But, what do we find? God is God (see Job). In weakness, we are strong, and God's glory is made known (see Paul). A bold, but impetuous disciple dies a martyr's death, but not before turning the early church on its head, and paving the way for all of us gentiles [sic] to join the family (see Peter). Joshua 1:9 becomes profoundly true. The ultimate tragedy, the Cross, becomes our greatest hope. It's a very, very long list, indeed. Ultimately, God is glorified by those who are faithful, in all circumstances.

And prayer becomes so much more than a Christmas wish list with results predicated on whether I have been naughty or nice. I believe prayer is much more about changing US—both in the singular sense, and in the communal context. The power of prayer in my illness, at least to me, was in the collective of family and friends, God's people, approaching the throne of grace on my behalf, and what that means to us as fellow believers and as a Christian community. I found great comfort in knowing I could pour my heart out to God, not so He would know what I was feeling or going through (He obviously had a pretty good bead on that already), but because that is what He asks us to do.

I had a great peace that whatever the outcome, renewed health or physical demise, obedience and submission were the keys to all good things, and the fulfillment of the ultimate purpose of my life—to glorify my Creator. And THAT is God's sovereign will, I believe.

I love you, so very much.

As always,

Dad

Acknowledgments

To all who encouraged and challenged me to write, I thank you – pieces of you are in these pages. You have made me who I am, my faith what it is, and my prayers what they are. My deep and abiding gratitude to...

Chalice Press, for creating sacred space for all kinds of voices, including young clergywomen.

Young Clergy Women International, for building a strong, caring sisterhood. Your solidarity and prayers buttressed this book.

Brad Lyons, President and Publisher, for taking a chance on my first book and on me. Your humor, encouragement, and graciousness brought joy to each step.

Gail Stobaugh, Publishing Manager, for your kind instruction and spirit toward all my questions.

Deborah Arca, Director of Marketing, for visioning this book's path and how it could be a beacon of blessing.

Cara Gilger and John Carey, for your beautiful editorial work.

Penelope Dullaghan, for creating the cover of my dreams and painting the world we know is possible.

Marge Barrett, for empowering and loving my voice to greater strength, and telling me I could do this. You always brought the perspective I needed.

My Wholly Writers group – Sarah Scherschligt, Brooke Heerwald Steiner, Lori Archer Raible, and Deborah Lewis – for hugging my words and very life in such a special way. I miss you.

The Collegeville Institute, for forming my confidence as a writer and illumining for me *why* I write. You are the first place I named my desire to write a book of prayers, opening in me fresh experiences of the Word as inspiration for my own.

Beloved professors at both Bethel University (St. Paul) and McCormick Theological Seminary (Chicago), for expanding, loving, pushing, and guiding me. Yours is deeply holy work.

Kathy Long Bostrom, for giving me the nudge I needed to finally compose a book proposal and for offering your prayerful, loving guidance in both my writing endeavors and life as a mother/clergy-couple/author.

MaryAnn McKibben Dana, for coaching me along the way, teaching me how a flexible, open heart leads to the best kind of journey.

Don McKim, for encouraging my writing with warm friendship and for giving me some of my earliest publication opportunities.

Jessica Bronston, Emily Erickson, Abby Mohaupt, and Steve Thorngate, for reading my manuscript seedling and offering exactly what it needed to grow and flourish.

First Presbyterian Church of Sioux Falls, for sparking and fanning the flame. You will always be my faith family.

Sanford's Pastoral Care Department, for mentoring me with humble love, guiding me in a ministry of compassionate presence, and teaching me to pray through the most raw and glorious of life's experiences.

Tai-An Presbyterian Church of Taipei, for opening my ears to God's call and the wondrous beauty of life.

First Presbyterian Church of Fort Wayne, for loving me and allowing me to love you. How privileged I was to be one of your pastors. Your place in my heart is more precious than you know.

Tim Braithwaite, "TJ," for bringing "Ash and Starlight" to be with your musical vision and heart full of love. You planted the piece that would go on to bear more and more fruit.

Tom Lehn, for shining. One day you'll see how your faithful brightness impacted so many.

Marsha Lehn, for the prayers we've shared together, the prayers you've helped me say, and the prayers you've spoken over me. Your very life is one gorgeous prayer.

Matt Braithwaite, for sharing my heart, blood, and spirit. You continue to give my soul both shelter and strength, brother. And no one can make me laugh like you do.

Tacey Eneboe Braithwaite, Mom, for embodying how to love everyone, look for who's forgotten, and stay steady on the journey with a brave heart. Your spirit has formed mine in countless ways.

Tom Braithwaite, Dad, for always being my first hug and first phone call. You modeled how to love God with all your heart, soul, mind and strength, to be a vulnerable leader, and a lifelong learner. I couldn't be more proud or grateful to be your daughter.

Eden and Simon, for keeping the soul of me alive. You are my two very best teachers. I love you more than the world can hold.

Jeff, for holding my hand and heart with every step. There's no one I'd rather walk beside on the pilgrimage. For you, with you, adoring you – all the way.

All my gratitude, all my praise, all my love, and all my awe to the God who weaves all ash and starlight into beauty – Creator, Christ, and Spirit.

Notes

Ash and Starlight
[†] An explanation of this composition's meaning can be found at https://ariannebraithwaitelehn.com/2015/05/23/ash-and-star-light/.

When I need to release and receive
[†] Julian of Norwich, Revelation 13, Chapter 27, Revelations of Divine Love (circa 1393). Julian of Norwich lived from 1342 to 1416.

When I cry for the world
[†] Widely attributed to St. Teresa of Avila (1515–82), but not found in any of her writings according to numerous sources, so probably written by someone else. Still, it's beautiful.

When I'm unsure and doubting
[†] Louisa M.R. Snead, lyricist, "Tis So Sweet to Trust in Jesus," 1882.

For Christmas Day
[†] This prayer is inspired by Ann Voskamp's blog post, "Why a True Christmas Might be Painful," at (in)courage, December 9, 2010, accessed at https://www.incourage.me/2010/12/why-a-true-christmas-might-be-painful.html.

Scripture References

My Own
Ash & Starlight

My Own Ash & Starlight

My Own Ash & Starlight

* *

My Own Ash & Starlight

* *

My Own Ash & Starlight

Other Books from the YCWI Series

Any Day a Beautiful Change
A Story of Faith and Family
by Katherine Willis Pershey

Bless Her Heart
Life As a Young Clergy Woman
by Ashley-Anne Masters and Stacy Smith

Blessed Are the Crazy
Breaking the Silence about Mental Illness, Family, and Church
by Sarah Griffith Lund

Faithful Families
Creating Sacred Moments at Home
by Traci Smith

Making Paper Cranes
Toward an Asian American Feminist Theology
by Mihee Kim-Kort

Sabbath in the Suburbs
A Family's Experiment with Holy Time
by MaryAnn McKibben Dana

When Kids Ask Hard Questions
Faith-filled Responses for Tough Topics
edited by Bromleigh McCleneghan, Karen Ware Jackson

Who's Got Time?
Spirituality for a Busy Generation
by Teri Peterson and Amy Fetterman